Godliness is Profitable

By Kenneth E. Hagin

Chapter 1
SUCCESS BELONGS TO YOU

But refuse profane and old wives' fables, and exercise thyself rather unto godliness. For bodily exercise profiteth little: but GODLINESS IS PROFITABLE UNTO ALL THINGS, having promise of the life that now is, and of that which is to come . . . Meditate upon these things; give thyself wholly to them; THAT THY PROFITING MAY APPEAR TO ALL.

— 1 Timothy 4:7,8,15

Paul plainly said, *"Godliness is profitable"* (v. 8). If anything is profitable, it pays off. Companies making financial reports to their stockholders list profits and losses.

Thank God there is profit from serving God. Living for God is not detrimental to a successful life. It is *"profitable unto ALL things."*

I think the Spirit of God knew there would be those who would say, "Well, yes, it will pay off in the *next* life. We may not have much to show in *this* life.

Here we wander like a beggar through the heat and the cold, but when it's all over, and we land on the *other* side, it will be different. There's a great day *coming* — after a while — when we've left *this* vale of tears and sorrow. There's a great day *coming . . . .*"

Well, thank God, there *is*. But Paul said, *"Godliness is profitable unto all things, having promise of THE LIFE THAT NOW IS"!* The life that "now is" is where "I is" right now *in this present world*. The life that "now is" is where "you is" right now!

[Brother Hagin gave the following prophecy at this point in his sermon: *"Take heed. Listen. Give yourself wholly unto these things. Success and victory belongeth unto thee. Defeat and failure will waylay thee at every turn of the road. Satan will stick up his ugly head like a serpent out of the grass to hiss at you and call you stupid. But rise up in faith and call the Lord blessed. So the crooked place shall be made straight, and the valley shall be filled with glory, and the mountaintop shall shine with His blessing, and you will walk in His blessing and be blessed and glad in this life."]*

Chapter 2
LIVING IN THE NOW

"Having promise of the life that now is, and of that which is to come." Having — having — having. That's present tense.

There is a life that *now is*, and there is a life that *is to come*. I'm more concerned about the life that now is than I am about the life that is to come, because the life where I "now is" is the one I'm living now.

If you listen to some people, you get the impression that all the promise we have is in the next life, primarily. According to them, "You can get saved in this life, all right, but after you're saved, that's about it. You've had it! You're left to the mercy of the devil.

You're left to the mercy of the world. You can't expect anything much here."

But that's not what Paul is saying to Timothy, a young minister! He said, "Yes, godliness has a promise of the life that is to come, but godliness is profitable unto *all things*." Not just to the spirit, but to the soul, the body, the material — all things.

There are at least four things that godliness insures. We will study these benefits in the following chapters.

Chapter 3
GOD PROTECTS US

First, godliness insures *protection*.

If you have property or anything of value, you protect it.

I was at my son's house and saw his dog, King, chewing on a shoe. I said, "Hey! He's got one of your shoes!"

"Oh, he's not hurting anything," Ken said. "That's an old shoe we threw away."

Ken wasn't protecting that shoe because it didn't amount to anything.

We belong to God! We amount to something! He protects us!

I like the account of the woman with the issue of blood who touched Jesus, and He said, *"Daughter, thy faith hath made thee whole."*

Mark's account goes into more detail and I usually preach from it. But I like something especially about Luke's account.

As Luke records the story, he writes that when Jesus stopped the procession toward Jairus' house He said, *"**Somebody** touched Me . . . . "*

Until she touched Jesus, that woman was a *nobody*. But when she touched Jesus, she became a *somebody*!

Jesus didn't say, "Nobody touched Me." He said, *"Somebody* touched Me!"

According to the Book of Leviticus, this poor woman with the issue of blood was in the same category as a leper. She was unclean. A leper had to segregate himself from other people. If somebody got close to him, he had to cry out, "Unclean! Unclean! Unclean! I'm unclean!" He was a *nobody*.

But, bless God, Jesus said, *"Somebody touched Me."* He transformed that woman from a nobody to a somebody. I want you to know, *you're* a *somebody*.

Somebody asked me, "What do you mean when you say, 'Brother So-and-so is a *somebody*'?"

I mean he's a child of God. I mean he's a son of God. I mean he's a joint-heir with Jesus Christ—an equal heir. I mean he's in the family of God. That's a *somebody!*

Jesus tells us we are somebody. We are the Body of Christ. The Bible tells us that.

Writing to the Ephesians, Paul

uses husbands and wives as an illustration of Christ and the Church: *"Husbands, love your wives, even as Christ loved the church, and gave himself for it"* (Eph. 5:25).

He went on to say, *"So ought men to love their wives as their own bodies. He that loveth his wife loveth himself. For no man ever yet hated his own flesh; but nourisheth and cherisheth it, even as the Lord the church: For we are members of his body, of his flesh, and of his bones"* (vv. 28-30).

No man has ever yet hated his own body: that has to do with husband and wife, and it is beautiful. But there's a further thought here, my friends, that I want to get over to you: We are the Body of Christ. We are His Body.

A man's wife is bone of his bone and

flesh of his flesh. And as Paul points out, we are bone of Christ's bone and flesh of His flesh!

Paul said that men were to cherish and love their wives. Then he said, *"This is a great mystery: but I speak concerning Christ and the church"* (v. 32). We are precious to Jesus.

What I'm pointing out to you is that if you have valuable property, you're going to protect it. You're not going to leave it out for the dogs to chew on.

And godliness is profitable unto ALL things.

Godliness guarantees or insures protection, for godliness is profitable unto all things. Read the 91st Psalm and learn about the protection that is yours.

Chapter 4
PROMOTION DAY IS COMING

Second, godliness insures *promotion*.

Consider what God did for Joseph because he stayed true. Yes, he was sold into captivity. Yes, he was put into prison. But God blessed him in Egypt.

Ordinarily, a man would become bitter after spending years in prison. But because Joseph was faithful, God promoted him and made him prime minister of the greatest nation of that day.

Did it pay to be faithful? Did godliness pay off? Did it pay to say "No!" to his master's wife when she tried to seduce him? Yes!

Remember this: Joseph spent

about 14 years in prison. Most men would have given up by then. But also remember this: God doesn't settle up every Saturday night. God doesn't pay off the first of every month — or the first of every year.

But I want you to know, brother, sister, that someday payday's coming!

We take that text from Galatians 6:7 — *"Whatsoever a man soweth, that shall he also reap"* — and we make an evangelistic sermon out of it. Yet Paul never wrote it to sinners; he wrote it to *Christians!* He wrote it to be read throughout all the churches of Galatia.

What he's saying to the Galatians is the same thing he said to the Church at Corinth, when he encouraged them to be faithful. He encouraged the Galatians not to faint, but to know that sooner or later they were going to receive the reward — the promotion — for their work in the Lord: *"Let us not be weary in well doing,"* Paul said, *"for in DUE SEASON we shall reap, if we faint not"* (Gal. 6:9).

That's the only way you can make it in ministry — by refusing to be weary in well doing. I completed 46 years of ministry in August 1981. I had every reason in the world to be weary. But I simply refused to be weary in well doing.

There were times when it didn't look like it was working. I mean, I preached faith when it didn't look like it was working for *me!*

I preached faith boldly, bless God, without a dime in my pocket.

I preached faith and prosperity

boldly with bills stacked up all around me.

I preached the Bible because I knew it was the Word of God!

I knew if I'd stay with it, sooner or later I was going to rise to the top.

If you think you're just going to float through life on flowery beds of ease, everything is going to come to you on a silver platter, and somebody is going to feed you with a silver spoon, you've got another thought coming.

God will promote you. Sure He will. But you're going to have to make the dedication and consecration. You're going to have to make the choice. You're going to have to have the intestinal fortitude that some people call guts to say, "This is what God called me to do, and I'm going to do it, go over or under, come hell or high water, sink or swim, live or die, burn every bridge behind me, praise God."

My wife and I made that kind of dedication. It looked like we were going to do all of it, too! It looked like we were going to sink. It looked like we were going to go under. It looked like we were going to die.

But I had meant it when I said, "I'm not going to turn back," because Jesus said, *"No man, having put his hand to the plough, and looking back, is fit for the kingdom of God"* (Luke 9:62).

Praise God, I knew this was it. I knew this was what God wanted me to do, even when it seemed nobody was listening. I preached this way when I was young, too. People would say, "You know, that Brother Hagin's an odd character. He's odd." And my friends would say, "Well, I don't understand him myself."

You see, you're an oddity to others when you walk by faith and they're all walking by sight. You're an oddity to people when you won't worry. You're an oddity to people when you're obeying God and preaching that God will promote you—and you have to sell your automobile for junk and light out on foot.

When that happened to me, I told myself, *Praise God, I'm not going to stop, even if I do have to junk that old car. I'm still going. If I have to walk to go, I'm still going. Because sooner or later, He's going to promote me!*

Chapter 5
TRUSTING FOR FINANCES

I have been many times afoot, with the soles worn out of my shoes, but I knew God would promote me if I'd be faithful. It wasn't that God withheld from me, but the devil was going to see if I really believed what I claimed I believed.

At every turn of the road, the devil will stick up his head. He's going to see if you really believe. He's going to put you to the test.

The same things could happen now that happened in the case of Job. The devil came up accusing Job. "Yeah, no wonder he serves You," the devil said. "Just look: Everything's nice. All of his children are well. He's got big crops.

He's got money. He's wealthy. Just take down the hedge and let me get to him. *You'll* see!"

Well, Satan's got a right to get to people here, because he's the god of this world. A lot of your transactions — especially when it comes to finances — are in this world, where Satan is god, and he'll really stick up his head.

But if you'll do what the Word says, you're not going to be afraid. I know. I know from experience. I can understand how Peter could lie down and sleep soundly when they were planning to kill him the next day. He was sleeping so deeply an angel had to smite him on the side to wake him up, and Peter didn't realize he was really awake until he got outside the prison (Acts 12:6-11).

But I understand that. The Lord has enabled me to lie down and sleep under the most adverse circumstances when nothing seemed to be going right. But I knew that godliness is profitable. I knew that if I would be faithful — if I would not be weary in well doing — in DUE SEASON I'd reap. I wanted to be there when the due season came!

Yes, it would have been easy to become weary. It would have been easy to quit. Absolutely. That would have been the easy way out: Just quit. Just give up. My flesh wanted to quit. My mind wanted to quit. But something on the inside of me — that Word and that Spirit . . . . Be a man or woman of the Word and of the Spirit.

Promotion will come, sooner or

later. It's coming. Be not weary in well doing, for in due season you shall reap if you faint not. Promotion day's coming. You're about to be promoted, glory to God.

Chapter 6
FORMULA FOR PROSPERITY

Third, godliness insures *prosperity*.

The Bible says that as long as King Uzziah sought the Lord, God made him to prosper (2 Chron. 26:5).

Furthermore, in the early days of Joshua's ministry, when he had to fill the shoes of Moses (think about having to fill the shoes of Moses), God told him exactly how to prosper:

JOSHUA 1:8
8 This book of the law shall not depart out of thy mouth; but thou shalt meditate therein day and night, that thou mayest observe to do according to all that is written therein: for then thou shalt make thy way prosperous, and then thou shalt have good success.

And right here in our text, Paul told Timothy, *"Meditate upon these things; give thyself wholly to them; that thy profiting may appear to all"* (1 Tim. 4:15). (In other words, everybody can see it.)

Chapter 7
PERPETUITY:
IN FATHER'S HOUSE

Fourth, godliness will insure *perpetuity.*

In the 91st Psalm God said, *"With long life will I satisfy him, and shew him my salvation"* (v. 16).

In Psalm 34 He said, *"What man is he that desireth life, and loveth many days, that he may see good? Keep thy tongue from evil, and thy lips from speaking guile"* (vv. 12,13).

In the New Testament Peter quotes that Psalm, *"For he that will love life, and see good days, let him refrain his tongue from evil, and his lips that they speak no guile"* (1 Peter 3:10).

The Bible teaches that godliness insures perpetuity.

EPHESIANS 6:1-3
1 Children, obey your parents in the Lord: for this is right.
2 Honour thy father and mother; which is the first commandment with promise;
3 That it may be well with thee, and thou mayest live long on the earth.

Teach your children that while they're small. I taught Ken and Pat that passage nearly every day. That's the reason we never had to take either one of them to the hospital. (Those are not "well days" when you're in the hospital.)

Of course, somebody always comes up and says, "I know So-and-so, and he was a preacher, and his boy died when he was 12 years old."

Well, that doesn't change the Bible. Maybe he was a good man. Maybe he loved God with all of his heart, but he didn't have the revelation of what we know.

You see, the Bible says, *"The secret things belong unto the Lord our God: but those things which are revealed belong unto us and to our children for ever . . . ."* (Deut. 29:29).

When it was revealed to me, I knew it belonged to my children as well.

Yes, I believe we can believe God for long life here. But John 3:16 says, *". . . whosoever believeth in him should not perish, but have EVERLASTING LIFE."* Now that's long life, isn't it?

Just because I leave this body is no sign I'm dead! I'm never going to die.

The Bible says, *"Whosoever liveth and believeth in me SHALL NEVER DIE"* (John 11:26).

(Of course, if Jesus tarries His coming, we will depart these bodies at physical death.)

Your loved ones are not dead. Don't even say they're dead. They just moved out of *this* house into *Father's* House. Glory!

Did the Psalmist David say, "Surely goodness and mercy shall follow me all the days of my life: and I will dwell in the house of the Lord *till I die"*? No, no, no! He said, *"I will dwell in the house of the Lord FOR EVER"* (Ps. 23:6). Forever! *Perpetuity*. That means forever and ever.

Godliness means live for God. It's profitable. It pays off in this life. In *this*

life! And in *the life to come*.
    Be determined. Live for God.